1 MONTH OF
FREE
READING

at

www.ForgottenBooks.com

By purchasing this book you are eligible for one month membership to ForgottenBooks.com, giving you unlimited access to our entire collection of over 1,000,000 titles via our web site and mobile apps.

To claim your free month visit:

www.forgottenbooks.com/free901583

ISBN 978-0-266-86621-3
PIBN 10901583

Historic, archived document

Do not assume content reflects current
scientific knowledge, policies, or practices.

A report of recommendations made to
the National Capital Housing Authority
for proposed apartment units
for low-income elderly occupants

AGRICULTURAL RESEARCH SERVICE
U.S. DEPARTMENT OF AGRICULTURE

This report was prepared by

Mildred S. Howard and W. Russell Parker

assisted by

Lenore S. Thye, Genevieve K. Tayloe, Joan C. Courtless, M. Frances Wolfe

Clothing and Housing Research Division
Agricultural Research Service
United States Department of Agriculture

HOUSING FOR THE ELDERLY

A Report of Recommendations Made to the National Capital Housing Authority for Proposed Apartment Units for Low-income Elderly Occupants

Low-rent public housing is recognized as a primary means of providing a decent living environment for low-income elderly persons. Surveys show that many of the elderly in both rural and urban areas prefer to, and do live independently, but the type of housing available often determines whether or not they can continue to do so. Attention of federal, State, and local governments is focused on meeting more adequately the specific housing needs of the aging.

The Public Housing Administration (PHA), whose program is for the benefit of low-income families who need assistance in order to be adequately housed, has increased its efforts in behalf of the low-income elderly group. Recently, PHA has liberalized the requirements for admission to low-rental units, so that more of the elderly can qualify for existing projects. PHA also is planning many new projects either exclusively for the elderly or with a high percentage of units for elderly occupancy.

In 1961, the National Capital Housing Authority (NCHA), the local public housing authority serving the city of Washington, D.C., planned to build three housing projects in which the majority of units were one bedroom apartments designed especially for elderly occupants. Upon the instigation of the NCHA, a request was made by the PHA for the consultation services of the Clothing and Housing Research Division (CH) of the Agricultural Research Service at nearby Beltsville, Md. CH was asked specifically to help translate and apply results of their research on the housing requirements of rural families to the design of kitchens and other activity and storage areas in these urban apartments.

The NCHA arranged for the CH researchers to visit 20 apartments in four existing projects, to discuss with the occupants the types and extent of household activities carried on and the kinds and numbers of possessions stored. One housing project was 25 years old; the others had been built more recently. Two were only 3 years old. The residents visited included 12 elderly couples and 8 single women.

The information gained from these visits was needed to determine whether the space standards developed by CH for activity and storage areas for rural housing could be adapted to the needs of the elderly in this metropolitan area. Also it was thought important to know, before formulating recommendations, what furnishings the occupants owned, their evaluations of their apartments, and what features they thought should be incorporated in apartment units for the elderly.

The findings and recommendations developed by CH and made available to NCHA are presented in this report, for any assistance they might be to those in other areas of the country who are responsible for planning low-cost housing for the elderly. This report consists of five parts: (1) needs and preferences of tenants visited, (2) general recommendations for activity and storage areas, (3) kitchen arrangements suggested for NCHA apartment projects, (4) study plans for two apartments, and (5) conclusion.

The two study plans, developed at the request of the National Capital Housing Authority, incorporate recommended storage areas, minimum kitchen arrangements, and other features considered desirable for housing the elderly.

NEEDS AND PREFERENCES OF TENANTS VISITED

Kitchens

Tenants of the apartments visited suggested improvements for the kitchen more often than for any other room.

Over half of the tenants expressed a desire for lower wall cabinets; only the first shelf of most of the wall cabinets was low enough to be readily usable. One tenant said she had to step on a stool and then on a chair to reach many of the items in the cabinet, and that some of her neighbors were not physically able to do this.

Some kitchens had, in addition to the wall cabinets, an open storage pantry in which the lowest shelf was about 30 inches from the floor. The tenants liked these pantries but would prefer to have doors on them. Some tenants had hung curtains on them.

The apartment type range, 2 feet or less in width, provided satisfactory cooking facilities. In some apartments, however, the range was located too near a curtained window, thus creating a fire hazard.

Desire for more counter space and base cabinet storage was indicated. Some tenants had added base storage units but these usually were not as convenient as they might have been had they been selected and arranged for in the initial planning.

The storage space provided was inadequate for company china. Some tenants had dishes stored on the top shelves in the kitchen cabinets. In nine apartments there were china closets, buffets or both in kitchens, hallways, and living rooms, to provide supplementary dish storage.

Doors on cabinets are desired, judging both from comments and from actions of tenants who had open kitchen cabinets. Towel-covered shelf contents were noted in several open cabinets.

A need for better lighting and more convenience outlets in the kitchens was mentioned by several of the respondents. Light colored walls and figured floor coverings that would be easy to keep in acceptable condition were also considered desirable by the tenants.

Dining Areas

Dining space in the apartments visited was either in the kitchen or between the kitchen and the living room as an extension of the kitchen. Several families whose only dining space was in the kitchen desired larger kitchens. These kitchens were obviously too small for comfortable dining. Dining areas in the newer units were larger and had windows and the tenants seemed pleased with the arrangement.

Results of a study on housing requirements of the aged, made by the Housing Research Center, Cornell University [1] emphasize the desirability of an outside view from the dining table, particularly for persons living alone. Daylight in this area is also important because the dining table is often used as a center for many activities during several hours of the day.

Living and Sleeping Areas

Living rooms appeared generally adequate in size for the one-bedroom, low-cost apartments visited, although heavy overstuffed furniture in some made the rooms appear crowded. A majority of the tenants had a television set, table radio, sofa or couch, easy chairs, living room straight chairs, footstool or ottoman, dining table, and occasional tables. Four tenants had desks; seven had sewing machines.

Windows in living rooms seemed adequate for light and views, but further consideration needs to be given to selecting types of windows that can be cleaned easily. One tenant said she would like to be able to clean the windows on the outside also, because she had difficulty finding anyone to do it for her.

Bedrooms were small and crowded. Space was not adequate to permit convenient or attractive arrangement of the furniture. All tenants visited had two or more dressers, chests, wardrobes, or vanities in addition to the bed. Measurements were not taken, but the bedrooms did not appear to be large enough to accommodate twin beds.

Some bedrooms were poorly located in relation to other areas of the building. One was next to a screened play area off a corridor, and the occupant of this apartment complained about the noise made by groups who gathered in the evenings. Other bedrooms located next to incinerators were too warm for comfortable sleep. Closets next to incinerators were too warm for satisfactory storage of clothing.

Bathrooms

Several tenants wanted a shower in the bathroom. Two suggested that with a rod and a shower curtain the tub could be screened off and two persons could occupy the room at the same time. Several commented on the inadequacy of the mechanical ventilation. Tenants liked the grab bars in the bathrooms; it was noted, however, that in one apartment the grab bar was coming loose from the wall.

Laundry Facilities

The combination sink and laundry tray provided in the apartment kitchens was very well liked.

When questioned about the group laundry facilities provided in the projects, complaints were voiced about the few washers usually in operating condition, lack of care of laundry rooms, and the disregard of some users for laundry of others found in washers or dryers. Some tenants said they preferred to use the commercial, self-service laundries rather than the project facilities. No doubt the popularity of the laundry tray in the kitchen can be partly attributed to the lack of satisfactory group laundry facilities.

---

[1] Cornell University, Housing Research Center. Housing requirements of the aged--A study of design criteria. 124 pp. Ithaca, N.Y. 1958.

Storage Areas

Many tenants suggested the need for more or larger closets, and mentioned specifically separate linen closets and larger closets in halls. One tenant suggested that better use could be made of the space in the bedroom closet if it were sectioned for the storage of shoes, hats, and bags. There was some dissatisfaction with sliding doors on closets because they did not work well. Tenants whose closets had no doors expressed a desire for doors.

GENERAL RECOMMENDATIONS FOR ACTIVITY AND STORAGE AREAS

Kitchen Equipment, Counter Areas, and Storage

These recommendations for kitchen equipment are based on the information gained from the people visited, and on the research findings and experience of staff of the Clothing and Housing Research Division. Also, the preliminary findings from the visits were discussed informally with NCHA staff, and their views and experience were considered.

Recommendations for work and storage areas are based on comparisons of the needs of the families visited with the needs of rural families for whom space standards have been developed and published. Some unpublished data were used also.

Sinks.--If laundry facilities are not provided on each floor of an apartment building, a combination sink and laundry tray, with removable drainboard, or a double-bowl sink is recommended for each apartment unit so that some hand laundering can be done in the kitchen. Thirty-two inch double-bowl sinks are adequate for this purpose and require less space than the conventional 42-inch combination sink and laundry tray. Stainless steel double sinks of this size are available with one bowl 7-1/2 inches deep and the other 10 or 12 inches deep, or with one bowl 3-1/2 inches deep and the other 7-1/2 inches deep.

If the double sink with one 3-1/2-inch deep bowl is used, the bottom of the sink provides a convenient work surface at a comfortable height for some food preparation jobs. Also, the worker may sit comfortably at this type of sink if the sink cabinet is designed with a shallow apron in front of the shallow bowl and the cabinet front is recessed. This is possible as drains on two-level sinks usually are set back of center.

Ranges.--A conventional range 30 inches or less in width is satisfactory for housing units planned for the elderly. Wall ovens and built-in cook tops are desirable if there is sufficient space for them as well as for the recommended counter areas. Wall ovens, depending on design, may be easier to clean than low ovens but require additional space, and the added cost may not be justified in public housing.

A conventional 30-inch range usually has enough space between burners for the projection of pan handles. If, however, the range is less than 30 inches wide, at least 12 inches of space should be provided between the center of the front unit or burner and the wall or obstruction of more than elbow height, to allow space for safe handling of utensils. Though not essential this 12-inch clearance is desirable for all surface cooking areas regardless of width. A counter area in the space between the side of the range and the wall contributes to the safety of the cooking area and is an added convenience. If there is no counter area between the range and wall, the wall should be covered with a fire-resistant material. In L- and U-shaped kitchen arrangements, a minimum of 12 inches of clearance is also recommended between the turn of

4

the counter and the center of the front burner or unit of all ranges. (Fig. 1) Aside from safety, an added advantage is that better use can then be made of the corner counter area.

Figure 1.--Minimum space recommended between turn of counter and center of front burner or unit.

A recommended safety feature on electric ranges is signal lights for the top units. Ovens should have a light-colored interior finish. A light in the oven and non-tip pull-out shelves are added convenience and safety features.

If wall ovens are installed the first rack position should be about 36 inches from the floor. For those models in which a separate broiler is below the oven, the bottom of the oven interior should be about 34 inches from the floor. For models in which the broiling is done in the oven, the bottom of the interior should be about 32 inches from the floor.[2] If the wall oven is placed too high there is danger of burning the arms on the open oven door, particularly for older people with diminishing strength.

Refrigerators.--Refrigerators in apartments planned for older residents should be upright, free-standing models. They require less stooping than do the undercounter type. A model with the door of the "freezing" compartment hinged at the side is more convenient to use and to clean than one with the door hinged at the bottom. Older women of average height find it difficult to reach across a bottom hinged door into the freezing compartment.

Counter Space.--A counter area at least 24 inches wide is needed in all kitchens as a mix or food preparation counter. If the counter extends around a corner, as in L and U arrangements, one of the segments should be at least 18 inches wide. For most convenience in preparing food, this counter area should be located between two of the three items of major equipment; that is, between sink and range, sink and refrigerator, or range and refrigerator. Storage space for packaged food supplies and canisters of sugar and flour should be provided above or below this mix counter.

[2]McCracken, E. C, and Richardson, M. Human energy expended in using built-in ovens at different elevations. Stove and Appl. Builder 21(2): 36-39. 1956.

A surface is needed near the refrigerator on which to place foods to be put in or removed. The mix counter, the drainboard top of a laundry tray, or the sink drainboard may be used, depending on the arrangement of the kitchen.

A heat-resistant surface adjacent to or within easy reach of the oven should be provided on which to place the hot pans taken from it. With a conventional range, the range top serves the purpose. With a wall oven, the surface cooking area is adequate if it is within easy reach.

Provision should be made for draining dishes. With a double-bowl sink, a drain basket can be placed in one bowl. A sink drainboard or the drainboard top of the laundry tray will also provide sufficient space for draining dishes.

Storage Space.--The size and arrangement of the kitchen area determines whether separate wall cabinets or separate areas in a single cabinet should be planned for the storage of dinnerware, glassware, and food supplies. Dinnerware is most conveniently stored near the sink and near the dining table. Food supplies should be stored in the mix center.

Mix utensils, pots and pans, frypans, and kitchen linens are usually stored in base cabinets. If they have fixed shelves, only the front portion can be considered convenient storage. If pull-out shelves can be provided, fewer linear feet of cabinets are required, since the entire shelf area can be counted as convenient and usable storage space.

In addition to shelf storage in the base area, drawers are needed for storing small equipment, silverware, paper towels, napkins, and miscellaneous items. The required number of drawers may be supplied in base cabinets that combine drawer and shelf storage or in one bank of drawers.

The space under the sink in limited kitchen arrangements is usually reserved for storing vegetables such as onions and potatoes, which do not require refrigeration, for dishwashing and housecleaning supplies, and for the trash basket. Shelves inside the cabinet or on the doors make the space more convenient to use.

In some kitchen arrangements, it may be necessary to add a floor-to-ceiling cabinet or pantry to provide the necessary storage space. Adjustable shelves contribute to the usability of this cabinet.

Dimensions for Storage Space.--Recommendations for the amounts and kinds of kitchen storage that might be useful in planning new NCHA projects were based on estimates of items in apartments visited, and on storage dimensions established in previous USDA and State research projects. Recommendations for sizing storage facilities are shown in tables 1 through 6 and are summarized below.

Wall Cabinets.--The recommended height for the top shelf of a wall cabinet to be used for storing frequently used items is 68 inches from the floor.[3] A shelf 72 inches from the floor can, however, be used for storing lightweight items that can be placed and removed with one hand, or for items infrequently used. If conventionally designed wall cabinets are hung with not more than 15 inches of clearance between the cabinet and the 36-inch-high work surface below, the top shelf will usually be within the recommended height.

---

[3] McCracken, E. C, and Richardson, M. Human energy expenditures as criteria for the design of household storage facilities. Jour. of Home Ec. 51(3): 198-206. 1959.

Table 1 gives the interior width of wall cabinets needed for storage of dinnerware, glasses, pitchers, and serving dishes. The table is divided into three sections. In the first, dimensions are given for three separate cabinets--one for dinnerware, one for glasses and pitchers, and one for serving dishes; in the second, for two cabinets; and in the third, for one cabinet where all dishes, glasses, pitchers, and serving dishes can be stored in one location.

Widths are given for cabinets which have three shelves (four surfaces) as well as for cabinets with two shelves (three surfaces). Stock cabinets and conventionally designed cabinets are usually equipped with two shelves. Inside widths are given because overall width will vary with design, material used, and construction. Shelves should be adjustable for greater flexibility in use. Suggested shelf spacing is given in Planning Guides for Southern Rural Homes.[4]

---
[4] See footnote 1, table 1.

Table 1.--Widths of wall cabinets needed for storage of dinnerware, glassware, serving dishes[1]

Number of cabinets and items stored	Surfaces	Inside width of cabinet[2]	Surfaces	Inside width of cabinet[2]
	Number	Inches	Number	Inches
3 Cabinets (12 inches deep):				
Dinnerware (8 each, large plates, small plates, sauce dishes, cereal bowls, cups, and saucers).	4	16½	3	20½
Glasses and pitchers (8 each, juice glasses, water glasses; 1 large and; medium pitcher).	4	18	3	22½
Serving dishes (3 platters, 4 bowls, 2 jelly and relish dishes).	3	14	3	14
2 Cabinets (12 inches deep):				
Dinnerware, glasses, and pitchers	4	35	3	39½
Serving dishes	3	14	3	14
1 Cabinet (12 inches deep):				
Dinnerware, glasses, pitchers, and serving dishes.	4	42	3	52½

---
[1] Adapted from Planning Guides for Southern Rural Homes, by Regional Housing Research Technical Committee. So. Coop. Series Bul. 58, 66 pp., illus. 1958. Unpublished data. USDA.
[2] Because of variations in construction of wall cabinets, inside measurements are given. Add construction requirements for type of cabinet selected to determine overall width.

Table 2 provides a similar analysis of the storage requirements for food supplies. Foods are grouped according to the location at which they are usually used first: mix, range, sink, or serving area.

Table 2.--Widths of wall cabinets needed for storage of food supplies [1]

Number of cabinets and items stored	Surfaces	Inside width of cabinet [2]
	Number	Inches
4 Cabinets (12 inches deep):		
Mix supplies (3 canisters, and 21 packages such as leavening agents and mixes).	3	25$\frac{1}{2}$
Range supplies (5 packages uncooked cereals and beverages and 12 cans of food).	3	9
Sink supplies (3 packages dried fruits and vegetables and 6 cans of food).	3	8
Serve supplies (7 packages, such as crackers, cookies, jellies, and pickles).	3	10$\frac{1}{2}$
2 Cabinets (12 inches deep):		
Mix and range supplies.............................	3	35
Sink and serve supplies	3	17
1 Cabinet (12 inches deep):		
All food supplies	3	51$\frac{1}{2}$

[1]See footnote 1, Table 1.
[2]Because of variations in construction of wall cabinets, inside measurements are given. Add construction requirements for type of cabinet selected to determine overall width.

Base cabinets.--Table 3 presents the storage space needed for kitchen utensils. To facilitate planning different arrangements, widths are given for three separate cabinets, two cabinets, and one revolving cabinet.

Illustrated (fig. 2) is a revolving cabinet with three shelves. The number, type, and size of utensils reported by occupants of the apartments visited were assembled from the CH laboratory and placed on the shelves to indicate the capacity of a cabinet of this design. Utensils owned were usually of family size, indicating that tenants had not made replacements upon moving from their former homes. The opening of this cabinet should be 16 inches wide. Clearance between the middle and lowest shelves should be 13-1/2 inches; between the middle and top shelves, 6-1/2 inches. The closure should be attached to the shelves.

Figure 2.--Revolving corner base cabinet with shelves.

Table 3.--Widths of base cabinets needed for storage of kitchen utensils [1]

Number of cabinets and items stored	Surfaces	Inside width of cabinet[2]	Extra storage in unit
3 Cabinets (24 inches deep, 36 inches high):	Number	Inches	
Pots and pans (coffee pot, 5 saucepans and pots, colander).	3	22½ (with sliding shelves, 18 in.)	---
Fry pans and lids (3 frypans and lids).	3	11	1 drawer 5 in. deep
Mix utensils and small equipment (3 mixing bowls, 6 baking tins, 2 baking dishes, 2 other items).	[3] 2½	29½ (with sliding shelf, 22 in.)	2 drawers 4 in. deep
2 Cabinets (24 inches deep, 36 inches high):			
Fry pans + mix utensils...............	2	36	2 drawers 4 in. deep
Pots and pans	3	22½ (with sliding shelves, 18 in.)	---
1 Cabinet (24 inches deep, 36 inches high):			
All fry pans, mix utensils	1 revolving corner base cabinet with 3 surfaces--1 with 10 in. radius, 2 with 18 in. radius (see p. 9)		

[1]See footnote 1, Table 1.
[2]Because of variations in construction of base cabinets, inside measurements are given. Add construction requirements for type of cabinet selected to determine overall dimensions.
[3]Half of space between top and bottom surfaces left free for file storage of baking pans.

Table 4 presents the drawer storage needed for kitchen linens, small equipment, and miscellaneous supplies.

Table 4.--Number and dimensions of drawers needed in kitchens for storage of specified items[1]

Item stored	Drawers	Inside dimensions[2]	
		Vertical depth	Width
	Number	Inches	Inches
Kitchen linens.......................	1 or 2	4 4	15 9
Silverware	1	4	9
Kitchen cutlery and tools	1 or 2	4 4	21 12
Miscellaneous supplies (such as paper towels, napkins, and wax paper).	1	5	15
Linens, silver, cutlery and miscellaneous supplies.	5	5	15

[1]Developed from unpublished data, USDA.

[2]Because of variations in construction of base cabinets, inside measurements are given. Add construction requirements for type of cabinet selected to determine overall dimensions.

Other Storage

Clothing.--Information secured from the families visited indicated that storage space for 50 garments was sufficient for two people. The rod space required for individual garments determined through research was used to calculate the total rod storage needed. In Table 5 the storage requirements are given separately for coats and outside jackets, since it is usually more convenient to store outer wraps near the entrance to the apartment than in the bedroom closet.

Table 5.--Length of closet rod and inside depth of closet required for storage of clothing [1]

Items stored	Length of rod	Inside depth of closet
	Feet	Inches
Women's clothes, 23 - 24 garments	3½	24
Men's clothes, 15 - 17 garments	3	24
Coats and outside jackets, 9 garments...	2½	27

[1] Developed from unpublished data, USDA.

Household linens.--The limited information available indicated that the types and quantities of linens owned by the elderly people visited in the NCHA projects were similar to those for which storage requirements had been developed by CH. Table 6 presents recommended dimensions for such storage in three separate areas, and in one combined area. Whenever possible, storage should be provided in the bathroom for some towels and other bathroom supplies.

Table 6.--Dimensions of facilities needed for storage of household linens [1]

Number of areas and stored items	Surfaces	Inside dimensions [2]		
		Side to side	Front to back	Between-shelf spacing [3] [4]
Three separate areas:	Number	Inches	Inches	Inches
(Bedding, curtains, washable rugs, 4 blankets, 8 pr. pillow cases, 8 sheets, 2 bedspreads, 3 pr. curtains, 2 cotton rugs).	5	26	20	14 (3) 8 12
Bath linens (8 bath towels, 1 bath set, 8 washcloths, 6 hand towels).	2 or 2	18 22	16 12	10 12
Table linens (3 table cloths, 8 napkins).	1	23	20	7
One combined area:				
(All bedding, bath, and table linens stored together).	5 or 6	32 33	20 16	10 10 (3) 8 (2) 12

[1] Adapted from Storage Units for Household Linens, by A. M. Woolrich and J. D. Herrington. U.S. Dept. Agr. Inform. Bul. 150, 14 pp. 1956.

[2] Because of variations in construction of storage units, inside measurements are given. Add construction requirements to determine overall dimensions..

[3] Space between surfaces. Numbers in parentheses denote number of surfaces with specified clearances.

[4] If pull-out shelves, drawers, or sliding trays are used, subtract 2 inches from each between-shelf spacing.

Cleaning and laundry equipment and supplies.--Brooms, mops, pails, and ironing boards were reported by almost all tenants visited, and half or more had wash boards and laundry baskets. Few families reported vacuum cleaners or carpet sweepers.

A cleaning closet 24 inches wide and 20 inches deep (inside dimensions) will accommodate three brooms or mops, one pail, one washboard, and one ironing board. There will be space also for a grocery cart or step ladder (these were reported by several tenants) or a vacuum cleaner or carpet sweeper. A shelf should be provided for cleaning supplies and the iron.

Bulk storage.--Some bulk storage space is suggested for each apartment. Electric fans, trunks, suitcases, and boxes of decorations, photos and mementos are the bulk items reported most frequently. No figures are presently available on which to base recommendations for storage of this category of possessions. A space 24 inches deep will accommodate an average size wardrobe trunk, and a space 18 inches deep will accommodate a man's three-suiter bag.

KITCHEN ARRANGEMENTS SUGGESTED FOR NCHA APARTMENT PROJECTS

Study by Clothing and Housing Research Division of the kitchen plans for three proposed NCHA projects revealed that the work and storage areas did not meet the recommendations summarized in the preceding section of this report. Since the plans for the three projects had progressed beyond the preliminary stage, dimensions and layouts of the apartments and areas within apartments had already been established and could not be changed. Therefore, plans for the kitchens were developed by CH within the space which had been allocated by the architects and which met PHA's minimum standards for space in one bedroom apartments in low-rent housing.

For Project A, two kitchen plans were developed. Figure 3 presents the preliminary plan of the kitchen included in the architect's drawings. Figures 4 and 5 are plan and perspective for a U-shaped arrangement suggested by CH which incorporates the recommended amounts of kitchen storage and counter areas. The sink and counters are arranged on two walls, and the refrigerator on the third wall.

A floor-to-ceiling closet 12 inches deep, providing storage for extra supplies and company china, is next to the refrigerator. A closure on this unit would be desirable, judging from the comments about open storage made by occupants in the apartments visited. A cleaning closet which opens from the entrance way backs up to this closet. However, this space, which also is 12 inches deep, will accommodate only a portion of the usual amount of cleaning and laundry equipment and supplies.

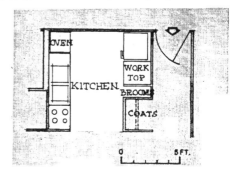

Figure 3.--Architect's preliminary plan for kitchen, Project A.

A conventional range is shown. Too much counter and storage space would have to be sacrificed if a wall oven and built-in cook top were used.

Figure 6 shows the plan suggested for a parallel-wall arrangement; figure 7, the perspective. In this plan the cleaning closet opens into the kitchen. However, space would not permit a cleaning closet of the recommended size.

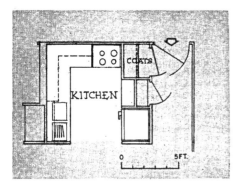

Figure 4.--U-shaped kitchen arrangement suggested by CH.

For Project B also, two kitchen arrangements were developed by CH. Figure 8 shows the architect's preliminary arrangement for the kitchen. Figure 9 presents a suggested U arrangement. The entrance hall was relocated to improve the circulation between kitchen and living room. The pass-through to the living room reduces the amount of walking between kitchen and dining table. If desired, the base storage space in the arm of the U next to the living room can be used from the living room side since the kitchen has sufficient storage without this space.

Figure 10 illustrates an L-shaped arrangement without a partition between kitchen and

Figure 5.--Perspective of U arrangement suggested by CH.

14

living room. The open plan gives a feeling of spaciousness but some means of shielding the kitchen at times might be desirable.

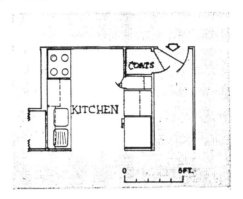

Figure 6.--Parallel-wall kitchen arrangement suggested by CH.

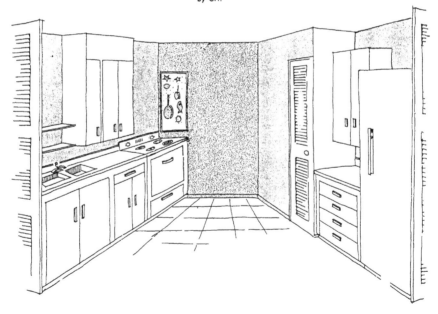

Figure 7.--Perspective of parallel-wall arrangement suggested by CH.

15

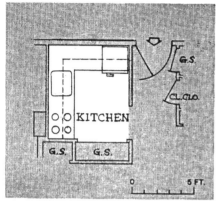

Figure 8.--Architect's preliminary plan for kitchen, Project B.

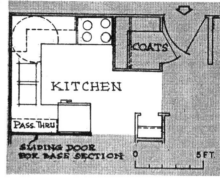

Figure 9.--U-shaped kitchen arrangement suggested by CH.

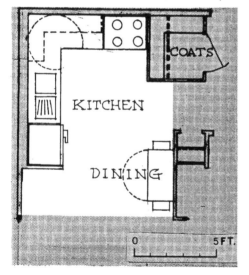

Figure 10.--L-shaped kitchen arrangement suggested by CH.

In Project C, the kitchen (fig. 11) was located at the end of and was as wide as the living room. Figure 12 presents the rearrangement suggested by CH. The width of the kitchen could be reduced to 9 feet 1 inch because a 32 inch sink rather than a 42 inch one was used. This permitted increasing the hall closets to the depths recommended. The length was increased to 6 feet to increase storage and counter area. The revolving base cabinet, shown in one corner, can accommodate all of the utensils listed in table 3, if properly designed. The undercounter space in the left hand corner can be used from the hallway for general bulk storage. A folding door could be used if desired, between the kitchen and the living room.

STUDY PLANS FOR TWO APARTMENTS

Because of the limitations of space and design of the three projects for which foregoing kitchen plans were developed, it was not possible to incorporate all the features that are generally accepted as desirable for dwellings planned for the elderly, nor to incorporate the recommended kinds and

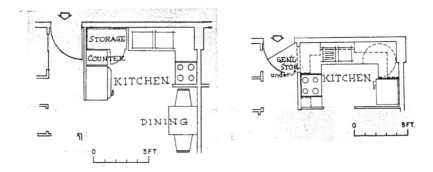

Figure 11.--Architect's preliminary plan for kitchen, Figure 12.--U-shaped kitchen arrangement suggested by CH.
Project C.

amounts of storage needed in areas other than the kitchen. Therefore, at the suggestion of the NCHA, two apartment plans were developed which included not only the kitchen arrangement but also location of activity areas, circulation between areas, and storage for clothing, linens, cleaning supplies, and bulk items.

Special attention must be paid to ease of moving about in dwellings planned for the elderly. Unsureness of gait, slowness, lack of balance, and unsteadiness of hand are the reasons for many falls among older people. Uncluttered passageways and easy accessibility between areas of the dwelling can greatly reduce accidents. The location of the entrance door in relation to the kitchen is particularly important. Many of the tenants visited had grocery carts. The grocery cart could be most useful for transporting laundry and cleaning supplies from one area to another if the arrangement of the apartment would permit its use. Handy storage for the cart should be provided.

In Plan A (fig. 13) the kitchen is located directly opposite the entrance to the apartment to facilitate bringing in groceries and other supplies. A cart can be maneuvered easily in this arrangement.

Clearance between facing equipment and counters is 3 feet, which is minimum for one person. To permit two people to work and pass each other, the between-counter clearance should be 4-1/2 feet.

The dining area is convenient to the kitchen as well as to the living room. If additional space is needed for company meals the table can be extended into the living room. The dining area is on an outside wall so could have a window.

The storage wall at the end of the living room, is conveniently located, and provides a buffer for hallway noises.

Access to the bathroom from all areas of the apartment is easy. In the bedroom, the dresser is located near the entrance which is convenient for daytime use. The room is large enough

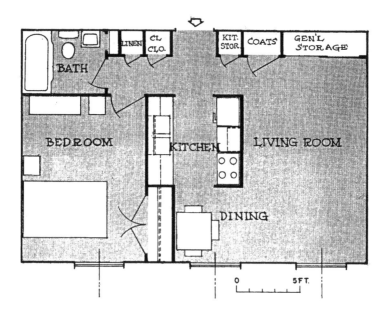

Figure 13.--Study plan A for apartment for elderly suggested by CH.

to accommodate a double bed with the recommended amount of space around it, but is not large enough for twin beds. According to a recent study on the space standards for household activities,[5] 22 inches is needed between beds and between a wall and a bed for bedmaking. Between the side of a bed and the front of a dresser, 48 inches is required for cleaning under the bed. Between the foot of the bed and the closet, 36 to 42 inches is needed for comfortable use of the closet. To conform to these standards the bedroom in this unit if furnished with twin beds, would need to be 15 feet 8 inches long rather than the 13 feet shown on the plan. It is wide enough to provide the minimum space in front of the closet.

In Plan B (fig. 14) the kitchen is located on the common wall between apartments to economize on plumbing. Between-counter clearance of 3 feet is shown, but a clearance of 4-1/2 feet would be desirable. Access to the kitchen, although not directly across from the apartment entrance, is convenient for bringing in groceries and other supplies, in a cart. The dining area is on an outside wall so it can have natural light and a view. The living room has enough wall space for attractive arrangement of furniture. One feature of this plan that might appeal to many is the door between the living room and the bedroom. Both the bedroom closet and the dresser are conveniently located for daytime use. The bedroom, however, is not large enough for twin beds if the recommended space is provided around and between them for cleaning and bedmaking. The room would need to be 14 feet 2 inches long to meet the recommended stand-ards with twin beds rather than the 12 shown.

[5]McCullough, H. E., Philson, K., Smith, R. H., and others. Space standards for household activities. Univ. of Ill. Agr. Exp. Sta. Bul. 686, 16 pp. 1962.

18

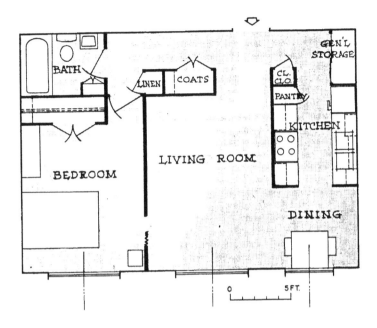

Figure 14.--Study plan B for apartment for elderly suggested by CH.

CONCLUSION

Although the information secured from the elderly tenants visited in public housing in Washington, D.C., was used, along with other data from research, in formulating the recommendations given in this report, it must be borne in mind that only 20 tenants were visited. This limited experience demonstrated, however, that elderly occupants can contribute many useful suggestions for improving their housing. It also indicated that systematic studies of representative families in different areas of the country are needed to reveal the types of housing problems that require further research and to serve as a basis for developing recommendations for nationwide use.

SELECTED REFERENCES

(1) Clothing and Housing Research Division.
1961. Beltsville energy-saving kitchen, Design No. 2. U.S. Dept. Agr. Leaflet 463, 4 pp. Rev.

(2) —————
1963. Beltsville energy-saving kitchen, Design No. 3. U.S. Dept. Agr. Leaflet 518, 8 pp.

(3) Housing and Home Finance Agency. Office of the Administrator.
　　1962. Senior citizens and how they live--An analysis of 1960 census data. Part I, The national scene. 20 pp.

(4) Howard, M. S., Thye, L. S., and Tayloe, G. K.
　　1958. The Beltsville kitchen-workroom with energy-saving features. U.S. Dept. Agr. Home and Garden Bul. 60, 13 pp.

(5) Richardson, M., and McCracken, E. C
　　1961. Energy expenditures of women performing selected activities while sitting and standing. Amer. Med. Women's Assoc. Jour. 16(11): 861-865.

(6) Thye, L. S., and Dodge, J. R.
　　1951. A step-saving U kitchen. U.S. Dept. Agr. Home and Garden Bul. 14, 16 pp.

(7) Western Region, Agricultural Experiment Stations, and Clothing and Housing Research Division.
　　1962. Space standards for home planners. U.S. Dept. Agr. Western Coop. Series Res. Rpt. 2. 16 pp.

Lightning Source UK Ltd.
Milton Keynes UK
UKHW020913220119
335965UK00013B/1891/P